WITHDRAWN

D1211549

Ypsilanti District Library

WITHDRAWN

Imitating *Nature*

From **Insect Wings** to Flying **Robots**

AUG 2 9 2006

Imitating *Nature*

From **Insect Wings** to *Flying* **Robots**

Toney Allman

KIDHAVEN PRESS
An imprint of Thomson Gale, a part of The Thomson Corporation

THOMSON
—★—
GALE

Detroit • New York • San Francisco • San Diego • New Haven, Conn. • Waterville, Maine • London • Munich

Ypsilanti District Library
5577 Whittaker Road
Ypsilanti, MI 48197

© 2006 Thomson Gale, a part of The Thomson Corporation.

Thomson and Star Logo are trademarks and Gale and KidHaven Press registered trademarks used herein under license.

For more information, contact
KidHaven Press
27500 Drake Rd.
Farmington Hills, MI 48331-3535
Or you can visit our Internet site at http://www.gale.com

ALL RIGHTS RESERVED.
No part of this work covered by the copyright herein may be reproduced or used in any form or by any means—graphic, electronic, or mechanical, including photocopying, recording, taping, Web distribution or information storage retrieval systems—without the written permission of the publisher.

Every effort has been made to trace the owners of copyrighted material.

LIBRARY OF CONGRESS CATALOGING-IN-PUBLICATION DATA

Allman, Toney.
  From insect wings to flying robots / by Toney Allman.
    p. cm. — (Imitating nature)
  Includes bibliographical references and index.
  ISBN 0-7377-3488-4 (hard cover : alk. paper) 1. Robotics—Juvenile literature.
I. Title. II. Series.
  TJ211.2.A46 2006
  629.8'92—dc22

Printed in the United States of America

Contents

CHAPTER 1

Nature's Flying Acrobats

Flies and moths are terrific fliers. They can zoom through the air, dart from place to place, and take off and land in a split second. Some scientists wondered if they could invent tiny robots with all the flying skills of flies and moths. Such robots could explore Mars, spy on enemies during wartime, or hunt for people trapped in the rubble of destroyed buildings. They would fly by imitating the high-speed flapping power of **insect** wings.

Fly Power

Two of the most common flies are houseflies and fruit flies. Houseflies are about a quarter of an inch (6.4mm) long. Fruit flies are only about an eighth of an inch (3mm) long. Both kinds of flies have two fragile wings that look too light and fine to hold up their fat little bodies, but these wings are very powerful.

Houseflies, for example, have seventeen wing muscles just for steering. With its strong muscles, a housefly

Moths demonstrate their amazing flying skills as they hover near a light bulb. The tiny fruit fly (inset) is also an outstanding flyer.

A Blur of Motion

Houseflies (below) beat their wings three times faster than hummingbirds do. Mosquitoes, which are members of the fly family, can flap even faster. Their wings beat an amazing 600 times per second.

can flap its wings 200 times a second. As its wings beat rapidly, a housefly speeds along at about 4.4 miles per hour (7 kph). That means it flies 300 times the length of its body in one second. A speeding jet flies only 100 times its body length in a second.

Fruit flies beat their wings as rapidly as houseflies, and they fly just as well. A fruit fly has amazing endurance, too. It can fly for six and a half hours before it needs to rest.

Zipping All Over

Flies are not just speedy. Both houseflies and fruit flies can make lightning-quick turns that are impossible for any other flying animal or plane. A fly can make a 90-degree turn in 50 milliseconds. (A millisecond is one thousandth of a second.) A fly turns faster than a human eye can blink. Scientists call these fast turns and direction changes **saccades**. A fly can zoom in a straight line or make many saccades without ever crashing, falling, or getting confused.

No matter how fast it moves or changes direction, a fly does not lose its balance. That is because tiny structures called **halteres** help the fly stay balanced in the air. Halteres look like tiny lollipops and sit behind the wings on the fly's body, or **thorax**. The halteres sense the fly's position much like **gyroscopes** keep airplanes balanced and flying in a straight line. With their halteres and fast wing beats, flies can turn loops in the air and even fly backward. A fly's reflexes are five times faster than a

A fly flaps its wings rapidly. The pictures below show one complete wing stroke of a fruit fly.

Nature's Flying Acrobats

Body of a Fruit Fly

Two fragile wings beat 200 times a second.

Tiny structures, called halteres, help the fruit fly stay balanced while flying.

The body of a fruit fly is only 1/8-inch long.

person's. That means that if a fly sees a flyswatter, it can take off so quickly that it is gone before the person trying to swat it can react.

Hawk Moths

Flies are not the only skilled flying insects. Hawk moths are expert fliers, too. There are 850 different kinds of hawk moths in the world. They have wingspans from 1.5 inches (40mm) to 7.5 inches (190mm) across. Their wings do not beat as fast as fly wings, but they flap about 85 times per second. With these large, flapping wings, hawk moths can fly 11 miles an hour (17.7 kph). They can also hover in one spot or dart and swoop from place to place.

How Do They Fly?

Scientists wanted to imitate the flying skills of flies and moths. If they could do this, maybe they could build robots that also zip through the air for miles, make lightning-fast turns, and hover in the air. Two scientists, one in England and another in California, decided to unlock the secrets of insect flight and figure out how flapping wings turn bugs into nature's acrobats.

Faster than a Speeding Bullet

Jerry Butler, a scientist at the University of Florida, tricked a horsefly into chasing a plastic pellet that he shot from an air rifle. The horsefly caught it. Butler figured out that the horsefly had been flying at about 90 miles an hour (145 kph).

CHAPTER 2

Flapping for Science

Scientist Michael Dickinson created a flight simulator for flies called the Rock-n-Roll Arena. It is used to study the way insects fly.

Insect flight is hard to analyze because bug wings move so quickly. At the University of California in Berkeley, Michael Dickinson set up experiments with fruit flies to learn how they use their wings to fly. Charles Ellington experimented with hawk moths at Cambridge University in England. The two scientists were determined to learn exactly how insect flight works.

Fly-o-Rama

In his laboratory, Dickinson built Fly-o-Rama. In this small tank, Dickinson could use high-speed cameras, which take 5,000 pictures a second, to record the flight paths of flies. He discovered that flies use saccades to avoid collisions. Each

Fly-o-Rama

Fly-o-Rama uses high-speed cameras to make a 3-D computer models of the flight pattern of a fruit fly.

Fabric enclosure

High-speed cameras

Infrared lights

3-D model of flight pattern

Fruit fly and its flight pattern

Digital signal processors

Video cassette recorders

Computer

Aiming for the Prize

Charles Ellington has spent his career working on a flapping robot. He once told a reporter, "It's always been my ultimate goal to have a little radio-controlled flying insect. I mean, that's what it's all about!"

fly needs only eight wing beats and a split second to make a saccade. However, Dickinson could not see exactly how the flies' wings moved. They flew too fast.

Rock-n-Roll Arena

So Dickinson built a small flight simulator, which he called the Rock-n-Roll Arena. The arena was a virtual-reality ride for flies. Dickinson glued a fly to a thin wire. A high-speed camera took pictures of the fly's wings as they beat and steered.

The Rock-n-Roll Arena was a little cylinder with moving pictures of stripes and squares on the inside walls. It rocked and rolled on a mechanical base. As the fly felt the movement and saw the landscape passing by, it was fooled into thinking it was flying. It beat its wings rapidly and aimed for a thick black stripe. The stripe looked to the fly like a countertop or table. It tried to fly to it and land. The cylinder rocked and rolled to throw the fly off balance. Using its halteres, the fly straightened its body and adjusted its flight path. The fly did not know that the wire held it still. The camera recorded every wing beat as the fly responded to the simulator. When Dickinson studied the pictures, he saw clearly how fly wings work.

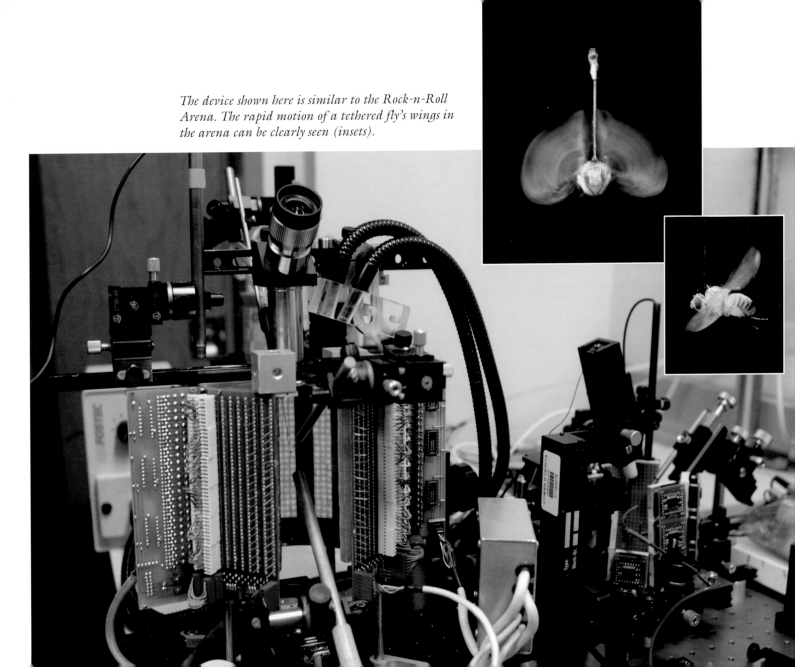

The device shown here is similar to the Rock-n-Roll Arena. The rapid motion of a tethered fly's wings in the arena can be clearly seen (insets).

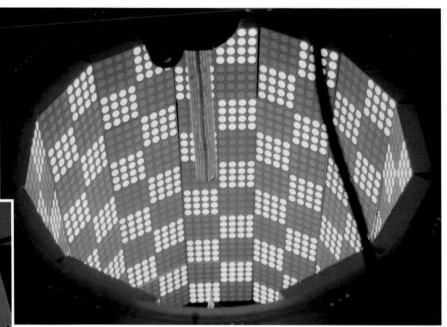

Flashing lights inside Dickinson's arena (right) trick the tethered fly into thinking it is moving.

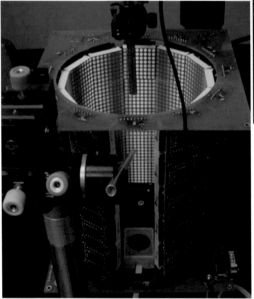

A Different Kind of Lift

Dickinson discovered that flies do not fly like birds. Things with wings stay airborne because of **lift**. During flight, air flows over a curved wing's upper surface faster than over its flat lower surface. This makes low pressure above a wing and high pressure below it, so a bird is lifted into the air.

From Insect Wings to Flying Robots

Flies have a different kind of lift. They flap their wings mostly from side to side instead of up and down, roughly in the shape of figure eights. The figure eights create lift by making little whirlpools in the air. The whirlpools catch the wings and lift the fly upward. With lightning-fast wing beats and halteres for balancing, a fly makes air whirlpools and steers through the air with ease.

Moths in the Wind

While Dickinson was learning about fly wings in California, Ellington was studying hawk moths in England. Ellington built a wind tunnel for moths. It was a small tunnel with a wind machine at one end and a place for the moth at the other end. The wind machine blew smoke at the moth, so Ellington could see the pattern the air made when the moth flapped its wings.

The moth was tethered at one end of the tunnel. When Ellington turned on the wind and smoke, the moth flapped frantically to stay aloft. High-speed cameras recorded its wing beats and the pattern they made in the air. Ellington's cameras showed that moths, too, make figure eights with their wings. Ellington

Virtual Fly Swatters

In the Rock-n-Roll Arena, Michael Dickinson made flies think they were about to be swatted so he could test their reactions. Without warning, a black square suddenly appeared on the simulator walls. Sometimes the square was on the fly's right, sometimes on its left, and sometimes directly in front of it. The tethered fly reacted instantly, making a lightning-quick saccade in the opposite direction. Dickinson had scientific proof that flies have incredibly quick reflexes.

said the whirlpools they make are like tiny tornadoes that suck up the wings and keep the moth flying easily.

Ellington and Dickinson now knew exactly how most bug wings work. Could scientific teams use this knowledge to make tiny flapping robots of their own?

From Insect Wings to Flying Robots

CHAPTER 3

Flying Bug Robots

Inventing flapping robots is difficult. Scientists have to imitate rapidly beating insect wings. The robots must have artificial muscles and extremely powerful tiny motors that can make figure eights and whirlpools. The first step is building model wings.

Robofly and Flapper

Dickinson and Ellington both built large models of insect wings. Dickinson's model is called Robofly. Ellington's is named Flapper. Robofly's wings are 15 inches (25cm) long.

The Micromechanical Flying Insect (left) being developed in Ron Fearing's lab is modeled on a real fly (right).

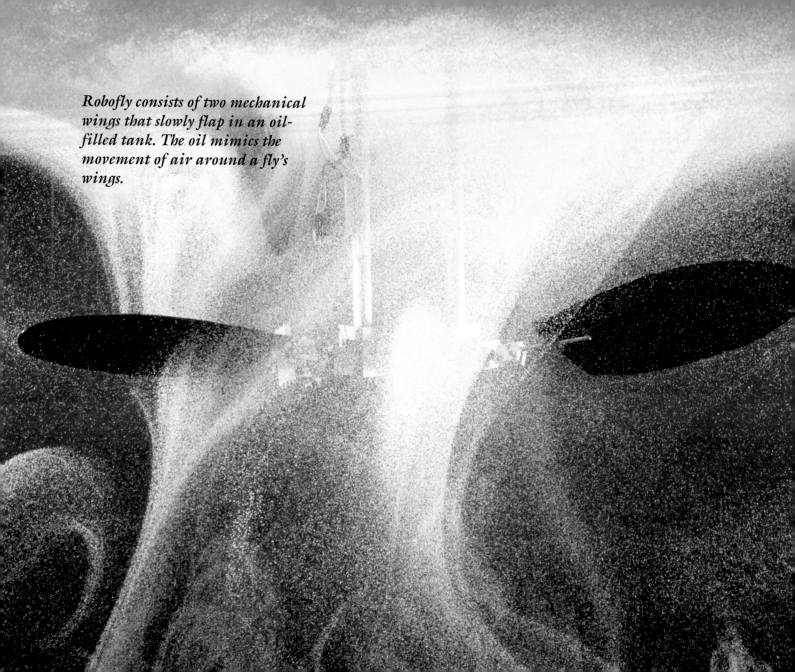

Robofly consists of two mechanical wings that slowly flap in an oil-filled tank. The oil mimics the movement of air around a fly's wings.

They flap inside a 2-ton (1.8 metric ton) tank of mineral oil. The oil mimics how thick air is to a tiny fly's wings. Robofly flaps its wings only one-hundredth as fast as real fly wings, but it imitates the figure eights that are necessary to create lift. Flapper's wings beat once every three seconds. Ellington can blow smoke at Flapper and watch the pattern mimic the flow of air over a hawk moth's wings.

With the experience of building models, Ellington and Dickinson were ready to join scientific teams and try to build real bug-size flying robots. Dickinson joined Ron Fearing, an **engineer** at Berkeley. Since 1998 Fearing has led the project to build a micromechanical flying insect (MFI).

MFI

In 2003 Fearing and his team built MFI—a robotic fly that is less than 1 inch (2.5cm) from wing tip to wing tip. It is made of a lightweight material called carbon fiber and has two thin polyester wings. Inside the thorax are tiny motors. Artificial muscles that flap the wings from side to side are attached to each wing. MFI beats its wings 150 times a second, but the motors

To the Rescue

MFIs would make skillful searchers during disasters such as hurricanes or earthquakes. They could fly into tiny openings in destroyed buildings or swoop into attic windows to look for survivors.

Beating Wing Power

A flapping lift-off takes more energy than driving up a hill. This is one of the challenges of creating flying robots. To drive up a hill at a speed of 60 miles per hour (100kph), a 2,000-pound (1,000kg) car needs a motor with 100 kilowatts of power (134 horsepower). By comparison, if a fly weighed 2,000 pounds (1,000kg), it would need twice the power of that climbing car just to lift up into the air.

are not yet powerful enough to make strong lifting whirlpools.

Without strong figure eights and whirlpools, MFI cannot fly on its own. It cannot create enough lift to get off the ground. Fearing says MFI has 90 percent of the lifting power it needs to fly. When it is lifted into the air, it flaps its wings and flies forward. Fearing still needs to invent more powerful tiny motors for the thorax. He also has to make gyroscopes that imitate halteres so that MFI will stay balanced.

Entomopter

Building MFI is difficult because making miniature parts with lifting power is so hard. Robert Michelson, at the Georgia Institute of Technology, and Ellington combined their talents to build a hawk-moth robot that is larger than MFI. It is called Entomopter. It has a wingspan of almost 6 inches (15cm) but weighs only 2 ounces (50g).

One model of Entomopter did have a successful test flight. It lifted into the air but not with a real motor. It

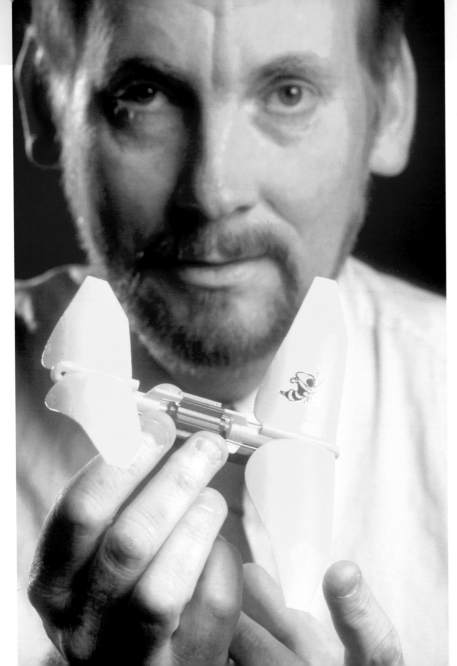

Scientist Robert Michelson holds his hawk-moth robot, Entomopter.

flew and flapped with a device similar to a rubber band. It could take off and buzz around, but it could not turn or control its flight path. Entomopter's fuel and motors have been tested separately and they do work, but now they must be made smaller and fitted into Entomopter. Only then will the robot fly like a real moth.

Flying Spies

Neither Entomopter nor MFI flies like an insect yet, but the sci-

Someday, an insect robot like this one may join NASA's rovers in exploring Mars.

entists keep working. Flying bug robots will be of great value to the military and to the National Aeronautics and Space Administration (NASA). NASA wants Entomopters that can go to Mars. There they will explore the planet, carrying cameras that send pictures back to Earth.

The military wants both Entomopters and MFIs. Flying bug robots would make perfect spies. They could fly into caves to search for terrorists or fly inside buildings to spy on people. An MFI could sneak up on an enemy tank, land on it, and leave behind an electronic detector. Soldiers could carry the little flying robots in their backpacks and release them

Mars Mission

NASA hopes to send several Entomopters to Mars on a spaceship. The agency plans to provide them with their own roving fueling station. The robotic station would be able to make its own fuel from the Martian surface. Then Entomopters would dock with it, refuel, and launch again for further exploration. Because Entomopters could land as easily as hawk moths can, no special runways for fixed-wing aircraft would be necessary. Entomopters would land on, and dock with, their base just as moths land on a plant or log.

In this illustration, an insect robot returns to its refueling platform on the Martian surface.

whenever they needed information about enemy movements.

Do Not Swat!

Scientists believe that tiny, flapping fliers such as Entomopter or MFI will be perfected by 2010. When that time comes, some of the insects that buzz through the air may be bug robots reporting for duty.

Glossary

engineer: A person who uses science and math to design, build, and operate machines, inventions, or structures.

gyroscopes: Devices such as wheels or disks that are mounted on a base, turn freely, and maintain balance and direction no matter what the base does.

halteres: The small knobs on a fly's thorax, behind the wings, that sense position and keep the fly balanced during flight.

insect: A bug that has six legs, three main body parts, an exoskeleton, and usually two pairs of wings. A fly has just one pair of wings and a pair of halteres.

lift: A basic aerodynamic force that operates in the gases of the air. Three principles of lift explain how things stay airborne. With one kind of lift, air flows faster across the curved upper surface of a wing than it does over the flat lower surface. Greater pressure is therefore exerted in an upward direction.

saccades: Extremely rapid turns made by flies during flight. A fly can rotate 90 degrees in less than 50 milliseconds.

thorax: The middle part of an insect body.

For Further Exploration

Books

Sara Swan Miller, *Flies: From Flower Flies to Mosquitoes (Animals in Order)*. Danbury, CT: Franklin Watts, 1998. Learn to be a fly watcher and to identify all sorts of flies. Houseflies, fruit flies, horseflies, and many others are described and pictured in this book.

Steve Parker, *The Science of Air: Projects and Experiments with Air and Flight (Tabletop Scientist)*. Chicago: Heinemann Raintree, 2005. Be a tabletop scientist with this book of experiments that students can do themselves. Learn what air is, why there is air pressure, and how lift works for airplanes and animals.

Web Sites

Entomopter Project (http://avdil.gtri.gatech.edu/RCM/RCM/Entomopter/EntomopterProject.html). Photos, animations, and videos of the Entomopter project are available at this site. The pictures alone are worth a look.

Fly-o-Rama: Dickinson Lab (http://journalism.berkeley.edu/projects/mm/spingarnkoff/flyorama/index.html). Follow the links along the top to find videos of Robofly in its mineral oil tank, Dickinson's flight simulator, and more.

How Airplanes Work: HowStuffWorks (http:// science.howstuffworks.com/airplane.htm). Learn about how airplanes fly and the aerodynamic forces of lift, thrust, and drag.

Yahooligans Animals: Insects (http://yahooligans. yahoo.com/content/animals/insects). Readers can explore the characteristics of insects, including different flies and moths. The site includes photos that help identify many common bugs.

Index

Picture Credits

Cover: Corel; © www.menzelphoto.com; Courtesy of Robert
    Michelson; Robert Michelson/Photo Researchers, Inc.
© Anthony Bannister/Photo Researchers, Inc., 8
© Sally Bensusen/Photo Researchers, Inc., 8–9
© Dr. John Brackenbury/Photo Researchers, Inc., 7 (main)
Courtesy of Michael Dickinson, 16 (main)
Courtesy of Mark A. Frye, 15 (all), 16 (inset)
© Dr. Dennis Kunkel/Visuals Unlimited, 7 (inset)
© www.menzelphoto.com, 12, 19, 20
Courtesy of Robert Michelson, 23
© Robert Michelson/Photo Researchers, Inc., 24 (inset), 26
NASA, 24–25
© Dr. Davis M. Phillips/VisualsUnlimited, 10 (photo only)
Photos.com, 18
Victor Habbick Visions, 13

About the Author

Toney Allman holds degrees from Ohio State University and the University of Hawaii. She currently lives on the Chesapeake Bay in Virginia and would love to buy her own robotic fly.